100 facts
Nocturnal
Animals

100 facts
Nocturnal
Animals

Camilla de la Bedoyere

Consultant: Steve Parker

First published as hardback in 2008 by Miles Kelly Publishing Ltd
Bardfield Centre, Great Bardfield, Essex, CM7 4SL, UK

Copyright © Miles Kelly Publishing Ltd 2008

This edition published 2010

2 4 6 8 10 9 7 5 3 1

Editorial Director: Belinda Gallagher
Art Director: Jo Brewer
Assistant Editor: Carly Blake
Volume Designers: Sally Boothroyd, Jo Brewer
Indexer: Gill Lee
Production Manager: Elizabeth Brunwin
Reprographics: Anthony Cambray, Ian Paulyn
Editions Manager: Bethan Ellish

ISBN 978-1-84810-235-4

Printed in China

British Library Cataloguing-in-Publication Data
A catalogue record for this book is available from the British Library

ACKNOWLEDGEMENTS
The publishers would like to thank the following artists who have contributed to this book:
Mike Foster, Ian Jackson, Mike Saunders
All other artworks from the Miles Kelly Artwork Bank

The publishers would like to thank the following sources for the use of their photographs:
Cover Frans Lanting/FLPA; Page 6 Frans Lanting/Frans Lanting PL/FLPA; 8 Tui de Roy/Minden Pictures/FLPA;
9(t) S D K Maslowski/FLPA, (c) Terry Whittaker/FLPA; 11 Kevin Schafer/Corbis; 12(b) Frans Lanting/FLPA;
13(b) NHPA/Martin Harvey; 14 Mark Jones/Oxford Scientific; 15(t) EcoView/Fotolia.com,
(b) Joel Sartore/National Geographic/Getty; 16 Tui de Roy/Minden Pictures/FLPA;
19 Audrey Eun/Fotolia.com; 20(t) Oxford Scientific, (b) Satoshi Kuribayashi/Oxford Scientific;
22 Cosi/Fotolia.com, (t) Roger Wilmshurst/FLPA, (b) David Cayless/Oxford Scientific;
23 Don Brown/Animals Animals/Earth Scenes/Photolibrary; 24 Fred Bavendam/Minden Pictures/FLPA;
26 Marian Bacon/Animals Animals/Earth Scenes/Photolibrary; 32 Jurgen & Christine Sohns/FLPA;
33(t) BIOS - Auters Watts Dave/Still Pictures, (b) Professor Jack Dermid/Oxford Scientific;
35 Mitsuaki Iwago/Minden Pictures/FLPA; 38(c) Animals Animals/Earth Scenes/Photolibrary;
39 Tim Shepherd/Photolibrary; 40 NHPA/Simon Booth; 41(b) Michael Quinton/Minden Pictures/FLPA;
42 Martin Dohrn/naturepl.com; 43 Deco/Alamy; 44 NHPA/Martin Harvey;
45(t) Malcolm Schuyl/FLPA, (b) Frans Lanting/FLPA; 47 Derek Middleton/FLPA

All other photographs are from:
Corel, digitalSTOCK, digitalvision, iStockphoto.com, John Foxx,
PhotoAlto, PhotoDisc, PhotoEssentials, PhotoPro, Stockbyte

Made with paper from a sustainable forest

www.mileskelly.net   info@mileskelly.net

www.factsforprojects.com
The one-stop homework helper — pictures, facts, videos, projects and more

Contents

1 Imagine standing in a forest as the sun goes down. Listen carefully and you will hear animals stirring and moving in the moonlight. Animals that are most active at night are called 'nocturnal'. From bugs to bears and bats to cats, there are thousands of animals that wait for the day to draw to an end and darkness to fall.

▶ The beautiful ocelot comes out at night to look for food. This cat lives in Central and South America and it hunts for birds, rodents, lizards and bats.

Super senses

2 **Nocturnal animals are mainly active at night.** This means they need super senses to find their way around in the dark. The darkness offers some protection from predators – animals that may want to eat them – but without great senses they would find it hard to search out food and mates.

▼ This maned wolf is sniffing the air trying to pick up the scent of its prey. Dogs' noses, or muzzles, are filled with smell-detecting cells. The black, leathery end to a dog's nose has two large nostrils, which pass the scents, or odours, over the smell-detecting cells.

3 **The five main senses are sight, hearing, smell, touch and taste.** Nocturnal animals usually have several or all of their senses heightened. These super senses are what help them to survive.

4 **Members of the dog family have an incredible sense of smell.** Some of them can detect odours, or smells, up to 50 times better than a human can. Wild dogs, such as wolves, coyotes, foxes and jackals, hunt at night. They use their large sensitive noses, or muzzles, to help them find their prey.

5 Raccoons not only have good eyesight for seeing in the dark, they have sensitive fingertips, too. These mischievous animals paddle in water, feeling under rocks for hiding crayfish, a type of shellfish. They use their long, agile fingers to grab the crunchy creatures before cracking them open to eat.

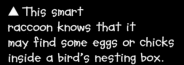
▲ This smart raccoon knows that it may find some eggs or chicks inside a bird's nesting box.

▲ A Malayan tapir is hard to see in the dark. It feeds on twigs and leaves in the forest.

6 Nocturnal animals may have super senses, but some of them have an extra trick to help them stay hidden from view – camouflage. Dull colours and dappled patterns on their skin or fur help them blend in with their surroundings. Malayan tapirs have distinctive coat patterns with black fur at the front and white at the back. This breaks up their outline and fools tigers – their main predators.

THE TOUCHY-FEELY GAME

Play this game to find out just how useful a sense of touch is.

You will need:
Two pillow cases
Small objects with different textures (rough, smooth, cold, furry, etc)
A friend

1. Each person must secretly place five objects in their pillow case.
2. Swap pillow cases with your friend.
3. Use your fingers to feel each object and work out what it is.
No peeking though!

Bright eyes

7 Finding your way in the dark is much easier if you can see well. Human night vision isn't very good and we find it hard to see anything in much detail without light to help us. Many nocturnal animals have astonishing vision and they can see a world of activity that's invisible to us.

▲ A tawny owl can spot tiny prey, such as mice, with ease. Its mottled feathers and dull colours help it to remain hidden as it hunts.

8 Most snakes rely on their senses of smell, hearing or touch to detect prey, but nocturnal tree snakes rely on their vision, too. They have narrow faces that allow them to clearly see what's right in front of them. Once a tree snake has spotted its prey, it folds its neck into an S-shape, focuses its eyes and then lunges with lightning speed. Its vision is so sharp, a tree snake can judge the distance to its prey with amazing, deadly accuracy.

▲ Vine snakes live in trees where they hunt their prey, such as lizards or passing birds. Their bodies are long and extremely slender and they have extremely good eyesight.

9 Tarsiers are odd-looking nocturnal animals that live in the tropical rainforests of Southeast Asia. They have enormous eyes and each eyeball is bigger than the animal's brain! Tarsiers can't move their eyes but they can swivel their heads 180 degrees in each direction, which helps them to hunt insects at night.

Light
Pupil narrows

◀ Tarsiers dart around the treetops in their forest home. As well as having amazing vision, they have good hearing, too.

10 Cats are well-known for their night-time hunting skills and owe much of their success to their eyesight. They have large eyes that are especially good at helping them to see at night. The pupil of each eye – the black part in the centre – can open up wide to let in more light in dim conditions. The back of the eyeball is coated in a mirror-like layer, which reflects light, making vision even clearer.

Darkness
Pupil opens wide

▲ The pupils of cats' eyes narrow and widen according to the amount of light there is.

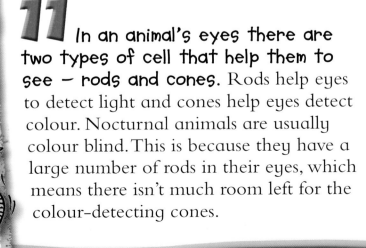

I DON'T BELIEVE IT!

Mammals are furry animals and have been around for more than 200 million years. Most were nocturnal until the dinosaurs died out 65 million years ago. With their major predators gone, mammals were finally able to come out in daylight!

11 In an animal's eyes there are two types of cell that help them to see – rods and cones. Rods help eyes to detect light and cones help eyes detect colour. Nocturnal animals are usually colour blind. This is because they have a large number of rods in their eyes, which means there isn't much room left for the colour-detecting cones.

Noises in the dark

12 Animals need to communicate with each other, and many do this by making noises. Communicating by sound is especially important to nocturnal creatures as noises carry well at night – a time when vision is not always so useful.

13 In the wild, night is not a quiet, peaceful time. The air can be filled with the screeching of owls, booming roars of lions and endless chatter of cicadas and grasshoppers. Animals that live in groups are described as being 'sociable', and nocturnal creatures use a variety of sounds to communicate. Some sounds are made using voices, while others are made by foot stomping and drumming.

◀ Grasshoppers have 'ears' on their legs or bodies rather than their heads. Males rub their wings or legs together to make noises.

▼ A lioness roars loudly to scare predators away from her cubs. Lions prefer to hunt in the cool of night.

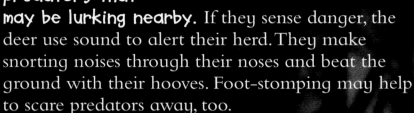

14 At night, white-tailed deer are on their guard for predators that may be lurking nearby. If they sense danger, the deer use sound to alert their herd. They make snorting noises through their noses and beat the ground with their hooves. Foot-stomping may help to scare predators away, too.

15 Crocodiles and alligators are impressive night-time hunters. They rest in the day, soaking up the sun. At night they become quick-moving creatures whose roars carry far across the still water. Male alligators make loud booming calls to attract females in the dark, but it's also been discovered that they can make rumbling low sounds that we can't hear.

▶ Bat-eared foxes have huge ears. They mostly eat insects and use their amazing sense of hearing to listen for beetle larvae gnawing through dung balls.

▲ A threatened crocodile hisses, bellows and roars before attacking.

16 Many nocturnal creatures have good hearing. Some have developed very large ears, or ears that can be moved to pinpoint noises better. Sound is 'caught' by the outer ear and then channelled through the ear canal to the hearing organ – the cochlea – inside the head. Sound information is then carried to the brain as electrical messages.

17 Many animals rely on their sense of smell far more than humans do and this is especially true of nocturnal animals. They use their sense of smell to find food, detect predators and find out about the other animals that are in their habitat — animals that may be hidden from view in the darkness.

▲ Kiwis tap the ground with their sensitive beaks to disturb worms and insects. They capture their prey by pushing their beaks into the soil. They also eat snails, spiders and berries.

18 Kiwis are rare, night-active birds from New Zealand and they have the best sense of smell of any bird. These fluffy birds have nostrils at the tips of their beaks and they use them to sniff out worms and other insects in leaf litter. Their eyesight is very poor, but they can hear well.

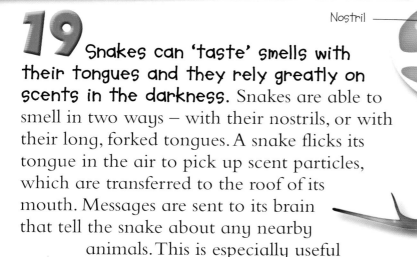

Nostril

Jacobson's organ

◀▼ A rat snake flicks its tongue in and out to pick up odours and transfer them to the Jacobson's organ, where they are sensed.

19 Snakes can 'taste' smells with their tongues and they rely greatly on scents in the darkness. Snakes are able to smell in two ways – with their nostrils, or with their long, forked tongues. A snake flicks its tongue in the air to pick up scent particles, which are transferred to the roof of its mouth. Messages are sent to its brain that tell the snake about any nearby animals. This is especially useful when hunting at night.

▼ Skunks have poor eyesight and can't see much further than a few metres in front of them. They use their excellent sense of smell to find food in the darkness.

20 Skunks are mostly active at twilight. These black-and-white striped animals spend the day in burrows and come out at sunset to look for food. They have a strong sense of smell and use it to sniff out bugs and small creatures such as mice and frogs. If threatened, a skunk sprays a foul-smelling liquid at its attacker – some say it's like a mixture of of rotten eggs, burnt rubber and garlic!

▼ A sloth bear's sucking noises can be heard up to 100 metres away!

21 By night, shaggy-haired sloth bears shuffle noisily through the forests in India. They hunt for termites and other bugs to eat and they find them using their noses. Once they pick up the scent of an ant or termite nest they rip it open using their long claws and suck up the tasty insects like a vacuum cleaner!

Feeling the way

22 Nocturnal animals often need a good sense of touch because it gives them extra information about their dark surroundings. Whiskers, hairy snouts, delicate fingertips and soft skin – there are many ways that animals can feel what's around them in the dark.

Whisker-like feathers

23 Frogs and toads have very sensitive skins and the natterjack toad is no exception. This nocturnal toad spends the day hiding under rocks and stones. At night it emerges to hunt for insects, spiders and worms. If it's disturbed by a predator, a natterjack toad can lighten or darken the colour of its skin to blend in with its surroundings. This helps it to hide from hungry hunters.

▶ Natterjack toads hunt for food at night. They can lighten or darken their skin colour to hide from enemies.

◄ Kakapos grow to a length of around 64 centimetres and they have small, useless wings. When they walk they hold their bristly faces close to the ground to feel their surroundings. Kakapos only breed every two to four years.

◄ A harvest mouse uses its sensitive whiskers to help find its way in the darkness.

24 **Kakapos are the only nocturnal, flightless parrots in the world.** Like all birds, they are very sensitive to touch, but kakapos have special whisker-like feathers near their beaks that they use to feel around. These, combined with their well-developed sense of smell, help the birds to find food, such as roots, fruit, nectar and fungi, in the twilight. Kakapos also give off a sweet-smelling body odour that may let other birds know they are there.

25 **When a harvest mouse creeps quietly through the shadows, it uses its whiskers to feel the way.** Whiskers are long, sensitive hairs. If a mouse pokes its head into a narrow space, it can tell by the pressure on its whiskers whether it can squeeze its whole body through.

26 **The brushtail possum has a big, bushy tail that is very sensitive.** At night when it becomes active, the possum holds its tail in the air and waves it around to feel its surroundings.

Brushtail possums live in Australia and many live in and around cities and towns. During the day they rest in tree hollows or even in house lofts!

► The underside of the brushtail possum's tail is hairless, which helps it grip as it climbs trees.

Night-time bugs

27 Insects and other bugs are amongst the noisiest nocturnal animals, especially in hot countries. An evening walk in a rainforest is accompanied by a chorus of clicks, buzzing, humming and chattering. These are some of the sounds made by millions of insects, which are invertebrates – animals without backbones.

▲ Common earwigs are insects that measure 8 to 18 millimetres in length. They are native to Europe, but are found in many countries.

28 Just like bigger creatures, insects and bugs use sound to communicate with each other at night. Cockroaches are leathery-skinned insects that are common throughout the world. Most spend their time scuttling silently through the leaf litter and twigs on the forest floor. However, the Madagascan hissing cockraoch can hiss if it's disturbed by pushing air out through its abdomen.

29 They may look menacing, but earwigs are completely harmless. By day they hide under leaves or in cracks and crevices. At night they come out to eat rotting plant and animal matter. They have pincers on the ends of their tails, which they use to scare predators away.

◄ Cockroaches can feel movement through their feet, which warns them to dash under cover to avoid predators.

▲ Feathery moth antennae can detect tiny scent particles.

30 **Moths have special organs on the front of their heads called antennae.** These long, slender or feathery structures detect smells and moths use them to find food and mates. These sensitive organs also help moths find their way in the dark. Moths with damaged antennae can't fly in straight lines – they crash into walls or fly backwards!

▲ Female moon moths produce a chemical that tells males they are ready to mate. Males use their antennae to pick up the scent of the female moths from several hundred metres away.

31 **Moths are some of the most elegant and beautiful nocturnal insects.** They have decorative patterns that help to camouflage, or hide, them. Members of the tiger moth family are often brightly coloured to tell predators that they are poisonous. Tiger moths also make high-pitched clicks to deter bats, which hunt by sound not sight. Once a bat has tried to eat one nasty-tasting tiger moth, it knows to avoid all clicking moths!

◄ There are many different types of tiger moth but most of them have fat bodies and brightly coloured wings. These warn predators that they are poisonous.

BED-SHEET BUGS!

Find out what nocturnal insects share your habitat.

You will need:
Large white sheet   torch   notebook and pencil or camera

On a warm evening, hang a sheet up outside and shine a torch onto it. Wait patiently nearby and soon insects will be attracted to the sheet. Take photos or make sketches of all the bugs you see so you can identify them later. Be careful not to touch them though!

Light at night

▶ Click beetles have two bright, glowing spots on their backs and one underneath their abdomen.

32 **One way for some nocturnal animals to deal with the dark is to turn on the lights!** Some of the most striking nocturnal creatures are fireflies and they light up by a process called bioluminescence (bio-loom-in-ess-ens). All sorts of animals can glow in the dark including insects, spiders, fish and worms.

▼ The flashing lights of fireflies are hard to miss, even in a dark, wet woodland. These beetles are also known as lightning bugs.

33 **If you're a small, dull nocturnal insect it can be hard to attract a mate.** Fireflies, which are actually a type of beetle, overcome this problem by flashing lights at one another. Tropical fireflies gather together and flash lights at the same time, making a spectacular light show. The lights turn on in patterns that vary according to the type of firefly. It's thought that firefly larvae may also use their lights to warn predators not to eat them.

34 Flashlight fish live where sunlight scarcely reaches — in deep water or caves. They have areas under their eyes called 'photophores'. These contain bacteria that produce light. The light helps the fish to see where they are going. It also attracts mates and lures prey in to eat. If a bigger animal comes too close, the fish flicks its light on and off before swimming away.

▲ Flashlight fish use their light to attract shrimps and small fish to eat.

35 Bioluminescence is a chemical process that happens inside an animal's body. Fireflies have special organs on their abdomens that contain these essential chemicals. When they mix with oxygen, a reaction occurs, making a sudden bright flash of light.

I DON'T BELIEVE IT!

Some crafty fireflies flash their lights to grab a bite to eat. They aren't after mates, but they fool other fireflies into thinking that they are. When the curious insect comes to investigate the flashing, they find themselves being attacked — and maybe eaten!

36 Bobtail squids have developed a bright way to forage for food at night and remain invisible to nearby predators. These animals can flash light around themselves, helping to hide their shadows as they swim. This clever trick is achieved with the help of some bioluminescent bacteria and some shiny plates that work like mirrors to reflect the light in lots of directions.

▲ Bobtail squids are small, soft-bodied animals that live in coastal waters, especially around Hawaii.

Coasts and seas

37 In water as on land, some animals choose to stay hidden from view in the daylight hours, but emerge at night. Many sea creatures live in waters so deep that light never reaches them and they live in constant darkness. In shallower water it is bright by day, but as the sun sets, many kinds of fish start their feeding and breeding.

▲ On wet, stormy nights, European eels can survive out of water for several hours.

38 The European eel is an odd-looking fish that can even travel across land. At night these long, snake-like fish may leave the water and slither across damp ground. They do this as they journey back to their breeding grounds to reproduce.

39 Horseshoe crabs are most active at night, mainly to avoid predators. They are called 'living fossils' because they have barely changed in 300 million years. They live in coastal waters but come to land to mate. These unusual animals wait until sunset before marching up onto the beaches where the females dig holes to lay their eggs – often several thousand each!

▶ Horseshoe crabs can reach 60 centimetres in length. They live in North America and Southeast Asia.

▶ Also known
as monkfish,
angel sharks are
heavily fished for
food and many types
are endangered.

I DON'T BELIEVE IT!

Lantern fish live in the deepest, darkest parts of the ocean. They become active at night and swim upwards — covering a distance of around 400 metres — to feed near the surface. Their bodies are so delicate that they die within a few hours if captured.

40 Angel sharks are night-time hunters.
Different kinds live all around the world and most grow to one to two metres in length. They were once common in the Atlantic Ocean and Mediterranean Sea, but now some are almost extinct. These flat sharks lie camouflaged on the seafloor during the day. At night, they swim upwards catching small, shelled animals and fish as they go.

▶ With their wide mouths and sharp teeth, moray eels make fearsome predators.

41 Moray eels are nocturnal predators.
They lie in wait for their prey, then ambush it. These long, thick-bodied fish rely on their sense of smell to detect other animals, so they can feed at night just as easily as in the day. They normally hide in cracks and crevices on the sea floor, but will emerge from a hiding place under the cover of darkness.

Dark depths

42 As darkness falls in the ocean, the world's biggest octopus comes out to hunt. The giant Pacific octopus can measure an incredible 7.5 metres from one tentacle tip to another. These extraordinary animals have soft, fleshy bodies and eight tentacles that are covered in large suckers.

▼ Ocean-living molluscs such as this giant Pacific octopus don't have hard shells to protect their soft bodies, so they need some impressive tricks to help them survive.

43 During the day, octopuses sleep in dens on the seabed close to land. They forage for food at night, searching for fish and shelled animals to eat. They kill their prey by biting it or pulling it apart with their tentacles. Sometimes, octopuses pour poisons onto the animal to soften its flesh, ready for eating!

I DON'T BELIEVE IT!

Female giant Pacific octopuses can lay up to 100,000 eggs at a time. They have 280 suckers on each tentacle, making 2240 in total. These monsters can swim to depths of 750 metres and can weigh as much as 180 kilograms!

44 **Southern stingrays feed primarily at night.** They have flat bodies that are almost invisible when lying on the seafloor. This helps them to hide from their main predators, such as hammerhead sharks. Stingrays have poor eyesight, but good senses of smell and touch, which they use to find crabs, shrimps and small fish when hunting at night.

▲ During the day, stingrays lie hidden from predators. However, should a predator come too close, stingrays have a deadly defence. Tey have tails equipped with sharp spines, which can pierce flesh and inject poison.

45 **Cuttlefish use colourful displays to communicate with one another in dimly lit waters.** These molluscs are able to change the colour of their skin in seconds, producing a range of beautiful, shimmering and metallic shades. This also creates an effective camouflage – a handy way to avoid being eaten!

◄ Cuttlefish, like squid and octopuses, are molluscs. These are animals without backbones that have soft bodies, and some types are covered with a hard shell. Cuttlefish may look a bit like giant slugs, but they are believed to be very intelligent animals.

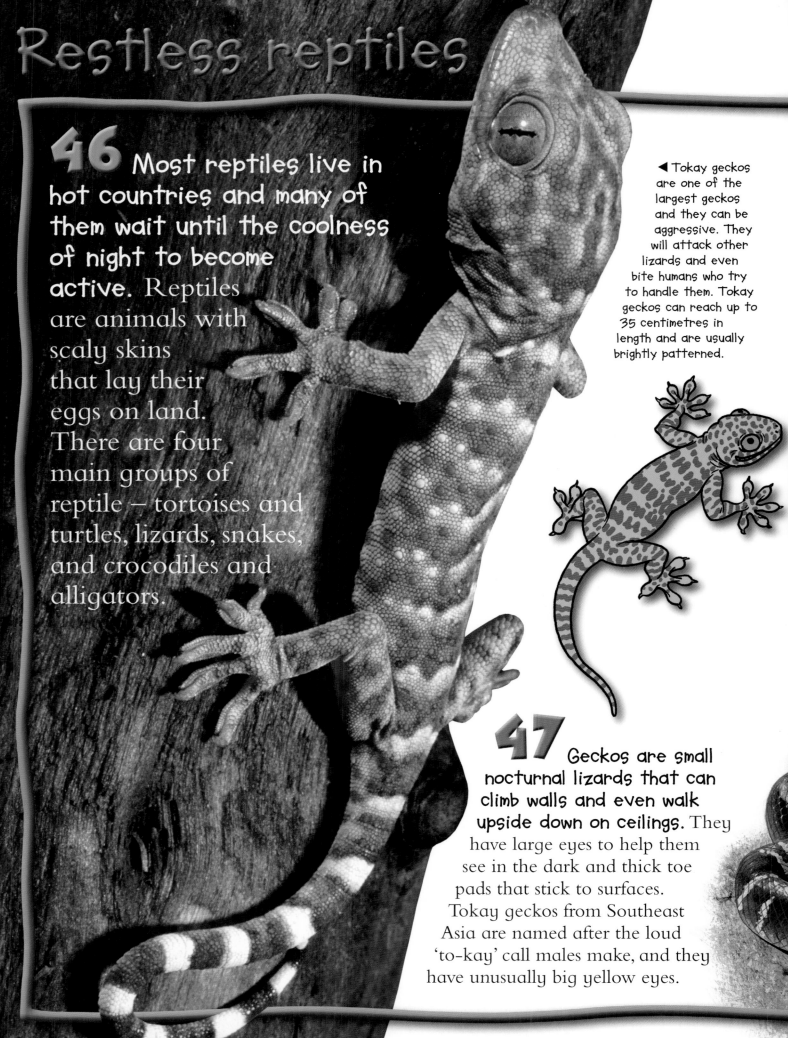

Restless reptiles

46 Most reptiles live in hot countries and many of them wait until the coolness of night to become active. Reptiles are animals with scaly skins that lay their eggs on land. There are four main groups of reptile – tortoises and turtles, lizards, snakes, and crocodiles and alligators.

◀ Tokay geckos are one of the largest geckos and they can be aggressive. They will attack other lizards and even bite humans who try to handle them. Tokay geckos can reach up to 35 centimetres in length and are usually brightly patterned.

47 Geckos are small nocturnal lizards that can climb walls and even walk upside down on ceilings. They have large eyes to help them see in the dark and thick toe pads that stick to surfaces. Tokay geckos from Southeast Asia are named after the loud 'to-kay' call males make, and they have unusually big yellow eyes.

48 Nocturnal snakes are superb hunters because their senses are so well adapted to detecting prey in the dark. Some snakes have an extra skill – they can feel the heat from another animal's body. Snakes, such as the western diamond rattlesnake, do this using special heat-detecting pits between their eyes and nostrils. Using this extra sense, the snake can find its prey in the dark and strike with deadly accuracy.

Heat-sensing pit

Body heat emitted from prey

The snake moves its head from side to side to locate its prey

▲ A western diamondback rattlesnake uses its heat-detecting pits to work out the distance and direction of its prey.

49 Some reptiles are huge and fearsome night-time hunters. Black caimans, which are members of the crocodile family, can reach 6 metres in length. They live in South America in freshwater rivers and lakes and at night they come to shallow water or land to hunt. Their dark skin colour means they can creep up on prey, such as deer or large rodents, unnoticed.

▼ During the day, common kraits are placid snakes and will rarely bite, even if disturbed. However at night they are more likely to be aggressive.

50 Common kraits are one of the deadliest snakes of Pakistan, India and Sri Lanka, and they are nocturnal. They prey on other snakes and rodents, sometimes straying into buildings to find them. Once they have found their prey, kraits lunge their fangs into it, injecting a lethal venom.

Whoo's there?

51 Owls are nocturnal birds of prey with superb vision and excellent hearing. Their eyes are large and face forwards, which helps them to judge distance. Their hearing is so good, they can locate their prey in total darkness just by listening!

52 The heart-shaped face of a barn owl works like a pair of ears! It helps to direct sound towards the sides of the owl's head, where the ears are situated at different heights. This helps them to pinpoint exactly where a sound is coming from. As they hover in the sky, barn owls can hear the tiny, high-pitched sounds made by small animals hidden in the vegetation below. Barn owls are able to fly almost silently towards their prey.

I DON'T BELIEVE IT!

Barn owls have white undersides, which may not appear to be the best camouflage for a nocturnal animal. This actually helps them to disappear against the sky when seen from below, allowing them to stalk and attack their prey more easily.

53 Barn owls are the most widespread land birds in the world and live on every continent, except Antarctica. They spend the day roosting (resting) in barns, buildings or trees and at night they come out to hunt. They catch rodents, such as rats, voles and mice.

▲ Barn owls have special adaptations that help them to hunt in the dark. Their soft feathers deaden the noise of flapping wings as they descend towards their unsuspecting prey.

54 Barn owls can see twice as well as humans by day and many times better at night. If an owl and a human were looking at the same image at night, the owl would see the image much more brightly. It would also be able to detect the smallest movement, which would be invisible to the human eye.

55 If they feel threatened or scared, owls slap their beaks together loudly making a clapping noise – this can sometimes be heard after dark. Barn owls shriek and hiss, but tawny owls are much more vocal. Their range of different calls can often be heard in the forests of Europe and Asia where they live. Male tawny owls make a loud 'hu-hooo' sound, which carries far in the still darkness. Females make a 'ke-wick' sound in reply. These noisy birds also make soft warbles and ear-piercing screeches!

56 Owls are the best-known nocturnal birds, but there are others that also use the cover of darkness to hunt. Many of them are so well adapted to life spent in the air that they can scarcely walk or hop. They sleep during the day, often roosting in trees, or hidden amongst plants on the ground.

▲ The gaping mouth of a nightjar acts like a net, catching insects as the bird flies.

▼ During the day, the common potoo mimics a branch to avoid the attention of predators.

57 Nightjars are stocky birds with big mouths that fly at night with their beaks wide open to catch insects. During the day, nightjars sleep on the ground or on low branches, without making nests. Their plumage – covering of feathers – is grey and brown, which camouflages them from predators, such as cats and foxes.

58 Potoos are odd-looking nocturnal birds from Central and South America. Their plumage is brown and they have yellow eyes. During the day they perch in trees, staying still with their eyes shut so that they may be mistaken for branches! At night, potoos dart through the sky gobbling up insects.

59 Few birds sing at night, but the nightingale's song can be heard floating through the darkness. The nightingale is known throughout the world for its beautiful song. Only male birds sing regularly after sunset and they use their songs of whistles, chirrups and trills to attract females.

◄ Frogmouths may attack and even kill other birds. They have very short legs and tiny feet.

▲ A nightingale's song is the only sign of this secretive bird's presence. Its dull colours keep it camouflaged.

60 Frogmouths are nocturnal birds from Asia and Australia that hunt on the ground. During the day they perch in trees, camouflaged by grey feathers mottled with dark stripes and blotches. A frogmouth's large, forward-facing eyes help it to spy prey at night, such as insects and small animals. Once prey is in sight, a frogmouth will pounce from its tree perch, capturing the animal in its beak.

HIDE ME, SEE ME!

Many animals are coloured or patterned in a way that helps them hide. This is called camouflage. But does it really work? Test it for yourself.

You will need:
thick, strong paper or card
paints or pens of different colours
scissors

Draw bold outlines of two birds. Colour one using bright, bold colours, but colour the other one in splodges of dull browns, greys and greens. Cut out your bird shapes and take them to a garden, park or woodland and hide them between plants. Which bird is easier to see?

Midnight marsupials

61 Kangaroos and koalas are marsupials, or pouched mammals, and most members of this group are nocturnal. There are about 196 types of marsupials living in and around Australia and about 85 types that live on the American continent. They are a strange group of animals that give birth to tiny youngsters that grow in a pouch on their mother's belly.

▼ Red kangaroos have a good sense of smell and they use it to find water in the Australian deserts.

62 Red kangaroos live in the great heat of the Australian outback where it's too hot for most animals to be active during the day. The red kangaroo is the world's largest marsupial. Its body reaches 1.6 metres in length and its tail is another 1.2 metres. It forages at night, nibbling at shoots, tender plants and leaves.

I DON'T BELIEVE IT!

Quolls are cat-like marsupials of Australia. They spend the night hunting, but during the day they like to sleep. Quolls find it difficult to nap if there's too much noise, so these clever creatures can fold their ears down to block out sound!

63 Koalas are bear-like marsupials that spend all day sleeping and all night eating. They eat and sleep up in the trees, and eucalyptus leaves are their main food. With stocky bodies, short limbs and leathery noses, koalas are easy to recognize.

64 Virginia opossums forage at night and survive on all sorts of food, including grubs, fruit, eggs and scraps they scavenge from bins. They live in North and Central America and shelter in piles of vegetation or under buildings. Opossums have an unusual skill – if they are scared they drop down and act dead, with their eyes and mouths open. They do this for up to six hours at a time – long enough for a predator to get bored and wander off!

▲ A Tasmanian devil gorges on its meal alone, but other devils may soon come to join in, drawn by the smell of fresh meat.

▼ A female Virginia opossum has up to 18 young in her litter, but she only has teats to feed 13 of them. She protects her young until they are old enough to fend for themselves.

65 In Australia's southern island of Tasmania, a terrible screeching and barking may be heard in the night – a Tasmanian devil. These marsupials are known for their noisy, aggressive behaviour and if they are alarmed, devils screech and bark. They can smell dead animals from far away and have such powerful jaws they can grind and chew bones and gristle.

66 Leaping between branches in moonlit forests requires excellent eyesight and fast reactions. These are qualities shared by many nocturnal primates. Lemurs, bushbabies, monkeys and apes are primates – intelligent mammals that have grasping hands and eyes that are set on the front of their faces.

▲ Owl, or night, monkeys are the only nocturnal monkeys of the Americas. They can see very well in the dark, thanks to their enormous eyes, but they are colour blind.

67 The only truly nocturnal monkeys are the night, or owl, monkeys, also called douroucoulis. Night monkeys have large owl-like eyes and small rounded heads. They feed on fruit, bugs, seeds and small animals. They howl, hoot and holler to communicate with one another in the darkness.

68 Mouse lemurs are the smallest of all primates and they are nocturnal. Some are only 18 centimetres long and weigh around 30 grams – about the same as four grapes! Mouse lemurs have very soft fur that is grey or orange-brown, with a black-and-white underneath. They live in trees and eat fruit, flowers, insects, spiders and occasionally frogs and lizards.

69

Bushbabies are small, furry animals that have huge eyes and can see well in the dark. They live in trees in the forests of East and central Africa. They run through the branches at night looking for insects, flowers, seeds and eggs to eat. During the day, bushbabies huddle together in hollow trees or sleep in old birds' nests.

70

As the sun sets on the island of Madagascar, the loud calls of ruffed lemurs can be heard across the treetops. These black-and-white, furry primates stay in touch with one another by making strange noises, which sound like someone laughing and screeching at the same time!

▶ Ruffed lemurs are most active at dawn and dusk, rather than through the night.

71

A slender loris uses all of its senses to guide it through the treetops at night. They are small primates that have huge eyes, nimble fingers and pointed noses. They live in India and Sri Lanka and they use stealth to hunt insects. A slender loris creeps up slowly and quietly behind its prey, sniffs its victim and then lunges, grabbing it in its hands.

◀ A slender loris measures no more than 26 centimetres in length and weighs around 300 grams. Its arms and legs are pencil-thin.

Beautiful bats

72 A flutter of wings and the glimpse of a swooping body in the night sky are often the only clues you'll get that a bat is nearby. Bats are the nocturnal masters of the sky. They are small, furry mammals that are so well adapted to life on the wing that they can pass by almost unnoticed by humans and animals alike.

▲ During the day, bats hang upside down and rest – this is called roosting.

73 Except for the polar regions, bats can be found all over the world. They roost in caves, trees, under logs and in buildings. There are nearly 1000 different types, or species, of bat – the smallest have wingspans of 15 centimetres, and the biggest have wingspans of 1.5 metres or more!

74 Bats are the only mammals that have wings. Their wings have developed from forelimbs and have a thin membrane of skin that stretches over long, bony digits, or fingers. Bats can change direction easily in flight, which helps them chase and catch insects.

I DON'T BELIEVE IT!

Bats can live for a surprisingly long time – often for 10 to 25 years. Some wild bats have been known to live to the ripe old age of 30! This is partly because bats are able to avoid being eaten as few animals can catch them when they dash and dart between trees.

75 Although bats have good eyesight, they depend more on their senses of smell and hearing to find their prey at night. Most types of bat have a special sense called echolocation. They produce very high-pitched sounds – too high for most people to hear – that bounce off objects in front of them. When the sound comes back to a bat's ears, like an echo, they can tell by the way it has changed, how far away the object is and its size.

76 There are two main groups of bat – plant-eating bats and hunting bats. Both groups are mainly nocturnal. However, it is the hunters that use echolocation to find their prey. Most plant eaters don't echolocate and tend to be bigger than hunting bats. Some plant-eating bats, such as the Rodrigues fruit bat, are active in the day. The word 'diurnal' (die-ur-nal) is used to describe creatures that are active during the day.

◀ The word 'sonic' means making sounds, and the high-pitched noises of bats can be described as 'ultrasonic' – too high for us to hear.

77 Oilbirds are unique – they are the world's only fruit-eating nocturnal birds, and they echolocate like bats. Oilbirds live in South America and they spend their days in total darkness, sleeping in pitch-black caves. They wake after sunset and travel up to 75 kilometres in search of food.

Echoes bouncing back off the moth

Sound waves from the bat

◀ Bats make high-pitched sounds, called clicks, using their mouths or noses. The sound hits an insect and bounces back to the bat's ears. The reflected sound gives the bat information about the location and size of the insect.

Insect eaters

78 Since many insects, grubs and worms are active night, so are the mammals that hunt them. Aardvarks are unusual ant-eating animals of Africa that snuffle and snort in the darkness. Their name means 'earth-pig' in Afrikaans, one of many languages spoken in South Africa, and they do look quite like long-nosed pigs with their big, fleshy snouts.

◄ Hedgehogs sleep during the day. At night, they come out to search for insects and worms to eat.

80 If they are scared, hedgehogs roll themselves into a tight ball with only their sharp spines showing. They may be able to defend themselves against foxes, but hedgehogs are no match for a car – thousands of these European mammals are killed on roads every year.

79 At night, aardvarks search for termites and ants using their good sense of smell as their eyesight is poor. They rip open nests and lick up the insects with their long tongues. Aardvarks also have large front claws, which they use for digging their burrows where they sleep during the day. They can close their ears and nostrils to stop dirt from getting in them as they dig.

◄ Aardvarks live alone and come out at sunset to forage for food. These long-snouted animals can eat up to 50,000 insects in one night!

81 Few people ever see pangolins as they are shy and secretive nocturnal creatures. Pangolins are armoured animals that live in Africa and Asia. Their bodies are covered in thick, overlapping scales, which are formed from layers of hardened skin. Pangolins don't have teeth, but lick up ants and termites with their long, sticky tongues.

I DON'T BELIEVE IT!

Armadillos are nocturnal, armour-plated relatives of anteaters. Their eyesight is so poor, they have been known to walk straight into the legs of people standing in their way! Armadillos eat almost anything they can find and have been known to dig into graves and munch on dead bodies!

▲ Pangolins have short legs and bodies measuring up to one metre in length. They can climb trees or dig burrows underground using their long, sharp claws.

82 Shrews are active by night as well as day, since they must eat every few hours to survive. They are mouse-like, furry creatures with long snouts and are some of the smallest mammals in the world. They rely mostly on their sense of smell to find food, but some of them use echolocation – a way of locating objects using sound that is used by bats and oilbirds.

◄ A tiny shrew prepares to devour an earthworm, which looks like a giant in comparison.

83 **Some of the world's commonest mammals are nocturnal rodents such as mice, rats, voles and lemmings.** This group of animals can exist in almost any habitat all over the world, except the Antarctic. They have big eyes to see in the dark, furry bodies, and teeth that are perfect for gnawing and chewing. Most also have good hearing, and long whiskers to feel their way in the dark.

▼ At night, rats roam around towns scavenging any food and scraps they can find.

84 **Rats are active in the day, but more so at night.** They are experts in survival – able to live almost anywhere. One of the reasons for their success is that they can eat nearly anything. Rats hunt for food but they are just as likely to scavenge rubbish from bins at night or find morsels in the sewers. These unpopular animals have been known to start eating the flesh of living things and spread deadly diseases.

85 Giant flying squirrels emerge from their tree holes at night and search for nuts, berries and shoots. They can 'fly' between trees by stretching out thin membranes of skin between their limbs, allowing them to glide through the air.

86 American beavers are large rodents, often measuring more than one metre in length from nose to tail-tip. They spend the day resting in a lodge, which is a nest made from mud and sticks with underwater entrances. Beavers leave their nests as the sun begins to set and they remain busy through much of the night, feeding on plants. They find their way around using their long whiskers to guide them.

▼ Beavers chisel at trees and branches, cutting them up for use in the dams they build on rivers and streams. These dams create wetlands where many types of animal and plant thrive.

87 Edible dormice are small, nocturnal rodents that live in woods, or make their nests near or under buildings. During the late summer and autumn they fatten themselves up with seeds, fruit and nuts to prepare for hibernation – a long winter sleep. The ancient Romans kept edible dormice and overfed them until they were so fat they could hardly move. They were cooked until crisp and crunchy and served at dinners and parties!

Death by stealth

► The serval is a member of the cat family that lives in Africa. Its large eyes help it to see prey in the dim light of the setting sun.

88 Hunting at night provides a perfect opportunity for carnivores to pounce on their prey, unseen and undetected. The word 'carnivore' describes meat-eating animals, and members of the cat family are amongst the most agile and elegant of them all.

▼ The glow from the eyes of these lions comes from the tapetum — a layer of light-reflecting cells that all cats have in their eyeballs.

89 Wildcats are the ancestors of domestic, or pet, cats. Like domestic cats, wildcats are active at night as well as during the day, but they do most of their hunting at night. They look like large, stocky tabby cats with black-tipped, bushy tails. They eat small rodents, rabbits and birds.

90 Many big cats choose the twilight hours — dawn and dusk — to look for food. Most live in places where the day's heat is too great for stalking and running. Cool nights are more comfortable for most animals, including prey animals such as antelope and deer that gather at waterholes or riversides. Big cats will sometimes lie in wait there — their tawny, stripy or spotty coats helping them to stay hidden in the shadows.

91

Leopards can hunt in the day or at night, but are more likely to be successful when the light is low. These strong, solitary animals are the most widespread of all big cats. Part of their success is due to their supreme hunting skills and the wide range of food they will eat. One clever leopard tactic is to ambush a group of baboons as they sleep at night – too startled to fight or run, the monkeys make sitting targets.

92

Wolves are carnivores and, like many other members of the dog family, they are nocturnal. Using their strong sense of smell wolves are able to detect animals, such as deer, moose, rabbits or beavers, and follow their scent trail for many kilometres. Wolves will always choose the weakest member of a herd to attack and they know to approach their prey from downwind so that it does not smell them!

▼ Wolves live in the far north, where night-time can last 20 hours or more during the long, cold winters.

43

The African plains

93 At dusk on the African grassland, diurnal (daytime) animals visit waterholes before resting for the night, and nocturnal animals become active. Hippopotamuses aren't everyone's idea of nocturnal creatures, but these huge mammals have very sensitive skin that easily burns in the hot sun. They spend the day wallowing in cool pools and come onto land at night to feed.

94 Hippos are plant eaters and spend the night chewing on plants at the waterside. They grunt and snuffle like pigs as they graze, eating up to 40 kilograms of plants and grass every night. Like lots of other nocturnal animals, hippos don't sleep all day, but have active times mixed with long naps.

▲ As the sun disappears behind the horizon, hippos amble onto the shore to graze on grass for most of the night.

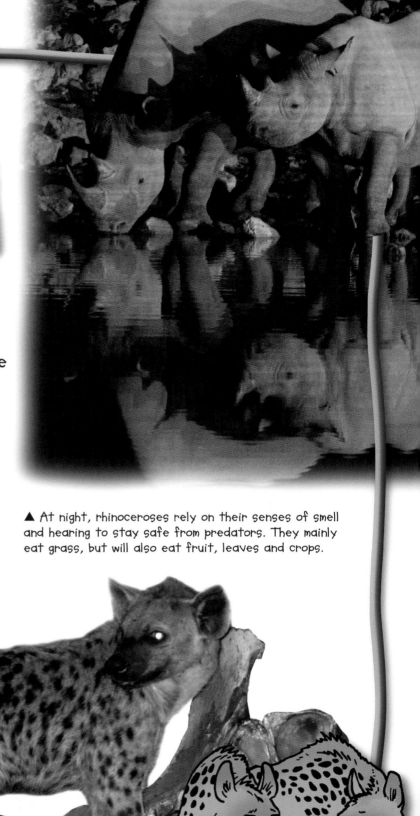

95 Rhinos are another animal of the African plains that prefer to feed once the sun has set and it is cool. These enormous plant eaters have poor eyesight and depend on their excellent sense of smell to find food and sense predators. By day they rest in the shade or bathe in mud to keep cool.

▲ At night, rhinoceroses rely on their senses of smell and hearing to stay safe from predators. They mainly eat grass, but will also eat fruit, leaves and crops.

96 Spotted hyenas are night-time hunters of the African grasslands. They are most active after dusk, and spend the day in burrows that they have either dug themselves, or have taken over from aardvarks or warthogs. Hyenas call to one another at night with a whooping noise. These calls show obedience to a senior member of the group.

▶ Hyenas can ambush and kill large animals because they work together in groups. They have excellent senses of sight, hearing and smell.

97 As night draws to an end, nocturnal creatures head back to their dens and burrows. Smaller animals steal away to hide beneath rocks, in caves or under plants. With their stomachs full it's time to rest and stay safe – and that means remaining hidden from view.

▶ Flying foxes, or fruit bats, are nocturnal plant-eating bats. During the day, they roost, hanging upside down by their feet from tree branches, in groups that sometimes number several thousand.

98 The break of dawn is a time of great activity and noise. Nocturnal animals are gradually replaced by diurnal ones. Birds announce the sunrise with their songs and bats can still be seen flitting around amongst the treetops, snatching insects out of the air. Lions laze around, having spent the night roaming the plains hunting, eating and napping. Cubs play in the cool air and perhaps wander to a waterhole to take a drink, before the whole pride settles down to a morning snooze.

WORD GAME

How many words can you make from the letters in the word NOCTURNAL?
You should be able to find the names of three animals that you have read about in this book!

99 Domestic cats are expert hunters and are most active in the twilight hours. Their well-developed senses of sight, hearing, taste and touch make them successful night-time hunters. They often return to their homes with small rodents, birds or insects they have caught in the night. Domestic cats usually spend the day sleeping and lazing around.

100 In rainforests and woodlands, morning dew drips from leaves as owls cease their hooting and foxes fall silent. Rodents scurry out of the light, seeking safety under stones or in cracks in tree trunks, and owls return to their treeholes. Now, diurnal birds of prey, such as eagles and hawks, hover in the sky, on the lookout for small rodents far below.

▼ European badgers snuggle together in their dens, called setts, to keep warm. They spend most of the day asleep.

▲ These young tawny owls have a safe place to hide during daylight hours. In this treehole, they are out of the reach of predators and protected from bad weather.

Index

Entries in **bold** refer to main subject entries. Entries in *italics* refer to illustrations.